Insider Guide

Getting Your
Ideal Internship

2nd Edition

Helping you make smarter career decisions.

WetFeet, Inc.

101 Howard Street
Suite 300
San Francisco, CA 94105

Phone: (415) 284-7900 or 1-800-926-4JOB
Fax: (415) 284-7910
Website: www.wetfeet.com

Getting Your Ideal Internship

2nd Edition
ISBN: 1-58207-331-7

Table of Contents

From Internship to Offer

- Overview

- Good Market/Bad Market

- The Bottom Line

Overview

Most people want to do what it takes to get their first choice in career opportunities or job placement. We are prepared to make the commitment in our job search to create the winning resume and the tailored cover letter, to sell ourselves in interviews, and follow up with thank-you notes and glowing references. What may be news to you is that, to really have an edge on directing your career options, the investment in your next job starts well before the job search. Each experience and skill you possess shapes the options that will be available to you later. That's where internships come in: They are one of the most effective vehicles for success in your career development.

Internships take you from where you are now to where you want to go. This is true whether you are just embarking on the first steps in exploring your options, are an experienced professional who is between jobs or considering a change in career direction, or are entrenched in a graduate or professional program and looking at how your training is going to play out in the working world.

The reason why is because no matter where you are now, internships give you additional skills, measurable accomplishments and experiences, and professional connections. And you are in the driver's seat: You can decide which internship opportunities will give you exactly the assets that will eventually get you hired.

What kind of internship should you pursue? Here are three simple steps to help answer that question: 1) Figure out the functional type of work you want to do (for example, marketing, finance, operations, IT, development, advocacy); 2) decide on the industry in which you'd like to work (transportation, health care, banking, high tech, social services, publishing, etc.); and 3) find out whether or not internships that fit your goals already exist, or if you will want to pursue your own avenues. Among other things, this guide approaches the question of "what kind of internship should I look for?" and provides you with the roadmap to find an answer and implement your course of action.

Here are some more compelling reasons to pursue an internship:

- Employers see internships as an extremely successful way to find qualified candidates.
- There are opportunities for internships in every field imaginable.
- By the time they graduate from college, many of your peers have already taken advantage of internships in developing their careers and marketability.

Take a look at some recent data from the National Association of Colleges and Employers (NACE):

- Employers responding to NACE's Job Outlook 2003 survey said they consider their own internship programs as the most effective method for recruiting new college graduates for full-time, permanent positions.
- Nearly 80 percent of respondents indicated they have an internship program. Manufacturers were most likely to have such a program (84.3 percent), followed by service-sector employers (80.1 percent), and government/nonprofit employers (56 percent).
- Overall, survey respondents said that more than 54 percent of their new college hires had internship experience, gained either with their organization or through another company.

Note: To find out more about the NACE Job Outlook 2003 survey, go to the resource section at the end of this guide, or visit the NACE website: www.naceweb.org.

So to reiterate: For many employers, internships are becoming an integral part of the hiring process. As you consider your career development, you'll find that for many reasons, internships are one of the surest ways to get on the inside track to your employment goals.

Good Market/Bad Market

Internships are a valuable tool whether you are planning your career in a tight economy or in one that is booming. When companies and organizations are slowing down recruiting efforts due to smaller budgets, reduced hiring/layoffs, or because they are serving fewer clients, it means that individual job applicants face much greater competition. The experience or skills you add to your resume as the result of a well-chosen internship will give you an advantage over your peers. Additionally, internships (or volunteer projects) are a fantastic way to avoid those "red flag" gaps in your resume if you are a career changer, or have lost your job. They allow you to continue to utilize your skills or develop new ones; they also show initiative, keep you active and engaged, and allow you to keep your professional skills fresh. Finally, internships grant you access to the "inside"—you are connected to the networks of people who are influential in hiring.

When the economy is flourishing, internships continue to be a good investment. Many employers offer internships because they see them as a great way to be involved in the community, to increase diversity in the workplace, and to test an intern for "fit" as a future employee. A good illustration of this comes from one major real estate services employer, who estimates that "one in eight company interns get actively recruited, and usually interns will accept the position if offered. These former interns get offered about 10 percent more than other new hires with equivalent experience from another company. Pay is higher for these new hires because we know they are reliable and do a good job." The "pretested" intern lowers the risks for the company. And, having encountered the company's daily activities, organizational structure, staff and current projects, the intern is able to make a better informed decision about their employment—and this of course leads to proactive and well-suited career planning.

The Bottom Line

Ultimately, a pillar of your success in finding or creating, and then leveraging your ideal internship will be your degree of focus. A tighter focus will help you hone your message. And the sharper your message is, the more credibility and sincerity your search will have—whether you are a former banker looking to get into corporate finance, an ESL teacher wishing to move into management consulting, or an undergraduate wanting to jumpstart an international career. If an employer is sold on your credibility, he or she will then be willing to make you an offer.

In this guide, you will find tools and information that will not only help you seek out and find internship opportunities, but create them as well.

Get Ready: Identifying the Value of Internships

- Do You Know What You Don't Know?

- Benefits of Internships

Do You Know
What You Don't Know?

When you apply to university or professional school, the application process is already mapped out for you. You are following someone else's plan as you take standardized tests, collect letters of recommendation, write essays, and have transcripts forwarded. Where in the application process does it say, "Figure out the type of job you'd like upon graduation, and find five people who've made a similar transition in order to pick their brains"? It doesn't. Know why? Because that should be part of the plan you draw up. In other words, it's *your* job to find a job. But without a plan, you'll be lost and will end up scrambling for career help only after the pressure and pain build to a level you can't ignore.

When preparing for school or for life afterwards, you should ask yourself these questions:

- What achievements or accomplishments am I most proud of?
- What are some of my strengths—personal qualities, skills, and abilities?
- What makes me most happy and fulfilled in my work?
- What is it about my work that I am most passionate?
- What types of people do I most enjoy working with?
- What kinds of growth opportunities do I look for?
- What new skills am I looking to acquire?
- What situations are most conducive to my learning?
- What types of challenges do I most enjoy?
- What work environment(s) promote my productivity?

Your responses to the above can reveal the extent of what you do and do not know about your career direction. Thoughtful answers to these questions form the basis for effective and successful career planning. If you can clearly, concisely, and enthusiastically provide robust responses to these questions, you are well equipped for a lifetime of proactive career development. You will pick positions and employers who are a better fit for you. You will do better in your interviews. You will be more directive in creating your next career opportunity. You will focus your time at work on things that you enjoy. And you will subsequently be happier in your career.

As you answer these questions, your responses will include details about challenges, environments, people, and opportunities. Are you guessing at these answers? If you're not sure, then you need to do some reflecting and investigating. It's best to talk with someone who has done, or is doing, the kind of work you're interested in, or to speak with a career advisor or counselor. A counselor can connect you with self-assessment resources that will help you clarify your skills, interests, goals, and focus.

As you refine, contextualize, and experiment with your responses to the questions, be aware of the impact these messages will have on potential employers. You don't want your responses to be dull, fuzzy, and rambling, or a recruiter will begin to wonder if you really know what you want to do. Sharp, clear, and concise responses are like gold to recruiters—they stand out and sparkle. After all, have you ever seen a job posting that didn't have "excellent communication skills" listed as a top qualification? Yup, didn't think so.

As you get a better sense of your career values and goals, you will become aware of where the "gaps" are in your skills or experiences. You may have already identified talents that you want to put to work, but perhaps not in the industry where you would be most engaged or comfortable. Conversely, you may be very happy with your field, but feel you need to build on current skills to move ahead. Begin talking with your peers, supervisor/mentor, and advisors about your responses to the questions above. Ask them for ways to gather the experience and skills that can initiate your move to your new career.

Bridging the Gap

Most people with broad gaps between their prior experience and future career field are probably not going to be able to fill the entire gap through a single internship. Instead, their best option may be to look for a "bridge" employer with whom an internship will cover a portion of the gap. For instance, take the case of a finance analyst with a large construction company who wants to move into a product development role with a pharmaceutical company. This person has two key elements he can leverage in making this transition: He has financial experience in a large organization whose work involves a tremendous amount of pre-planning, detailed work that's broken down into multiple phases and sub-projects, with long timelines to completion. And the industry he's in is linked to numerous other industries that involve product development—mainly equipment and materials manufacturers. The picture of where this person is and where he wants to go looks like this:

Prior Experience	Best "Bridge" Internship Options	Goal for Full-Time Work
• Financial analysis • Pre-planning • Detailed work • Multiple phases • Long timelines	1. Product development with an equipment or materials manufacturer 2. Financial analysis with a pharmaceutical company	• Product development • Pharmaceutical company

Though only two "bridge" options are presented, others are available to him. In fact, most people have numerous "bridges" they can take advantage of to ultimately land the job they want. A career advisor can help you find out what they are.

Benefits of Internships

Why is an internship the way to go? For those of us who are exploring their options, internships are a great opportunity to get a taste of work in a particular field of interest. For people who have narrowed their focus or career goals, internships provide an effective means to fill in the gaps between where you have been and where you want to go. This has to do with honing skills, developing experience, and investing in connections that will help place you with the employer(s) of your choosing.

Skill Building

Hands-on experience will allow you to build marketable skills. Your internship will give you the opportunity to choose what skills you will develop, creating a foundation of skills that will tailor your abilities to the career you are pursuing. Additionally, inherent in any internship is the chance to work on professionalism, communication, teamwork, project ownership and initiative.

What qualities do employers want most from the college students they consider candidates for employment? Employers responding to the National Association of Colleges and Employers' (NACE) *Job Outlook* 2003 survey were asked to rate the importance of candidate qualities and skills on a five-point scale, with five being "extremely important" and one being "not important." Communication skills (4.7 average), honesty/integrity (4.7), teamwork skills (4.6), interpersonal skills (4.5), motivation/initiative (4.5), and strong work ethic (4.5) were the most desired characteristics.

Note: To find out more about the NACE Job Outlook 2003 survey, go to the resource section at the end of this guide, or visit the NACE website: www.naceweb.org.

Of course, content skills are built through internships as well. Some major skill areas are administrative, analytical, coaching, management, and research skills. It's up to you to find out which skills are most valued in the field you are pursuing, and find an internship that will allow you to cultivate and demonstrate those skills.

Industry Exposure

Learn what it's really like to be in the industry, field, or company of your dreams. You will gain insights and understanding that you couldn't by research alone. The exposure derived from internships can teach you how the company is positioned in the industry, who the big players are, and what are the latest trends or industry forecasts.

Networking, Mentoring, and References

How many times have you heard "it's who you know" that gets you access to jobs? Your internship supervisors, coworkers, and fellow interns all have connections that will help you learn about the "hidden" job market. You have the opportunity to get acquainted with people who know real inside information about the nature of the work, future projects and areas of growth. At the same time, these colleagues can see firsthand the quality of your work and your enthusiasm. The contacts you make through your internship may end up being your advocates when it comes time for you to seek a permanent position. Any successful internship will strengthen your potential to make contacts with people who are in a position to hire.

Additionally, inherent in an internship is the understanding that both interns and employers are profiting by the position. Employers benefit as you help complete projects that add value to the company or organization. They also profit because they can groom future employees.

Interns benefit as well, not just because they can position themselves as future hires, but because internships are training experiences—a good internship will challenge you to master new skills and learn from your projects. This is best facilitated with effective management, clear goals, and evaluations during and at the end of the internship. Establishing positive relations with your supervisor will facilitate these goals. Take advantage of the training nature of internships to ask thoughtful questions and demonstrate your interests. Even if your internship does not lead to future placement within the organization, you may rely on the relationships you've established as a source of valuable recommendations or references for your next career move.

Academic Credit

Many schools will offer academic credit for approved internships related to your area of studies. Check with your career center and academic advisors. Generally, to receive credit for an internship, you must get approval prior to starting the internship. Find out from your advisors what the grading procedures are and the requirements you must meet to gain credit. Factors for eligibility may include the time you'll spend in the internship, the nature of the internship projects, supervision, and evaluations.

Compensation

Salary for interns can vary from hourly wages, pay by project, a set stipend, or no monetary compensation at all. The amount you get paid will also vary by field/industry, the amount of experience or educational level you have, and whether or not you are returning to a company where you have interned in the past. The bottom line is that you probably shouldn't expect to get wealthy from your internship, no matter the field you are pursuing.

Should you accept an internship that doesn't seem financially rewarding? Pride can sometimes hold you back. Particularly when that pride keeps you from accepting an opportunity to acquire some fantastic, or even moderate, experience because no pay is involved. Unthinkable, you say. What's the payoff if there's no money involved? However, think back to how wide a gap you have between where you've been and where you want to go. The wider the gap, the more willing you should be to work without pay in order to get the kind of experience that will build a bridge across your career gap.

Still not convinced? Let's take experience out of the equation. Instead, consider this scenario: You have six years of strong operational and managerial experience in small, locally owned and operated manufacturing businesses. Your career goal is to land a manufacturing management job with a Fortune 100 heavy equipment organization. So, let's say you've managed to receive an internship offer to work for a Fortune 100 employer. Now here's the question to test your pride: "How much would you actually *pay* to get the internship experience and exposure being offered to you with a Fortune 100 employer?" Keep in mind that snagging this plum internship could get you the job of your dreams. A-ha! Accepting the position even if it's unpaid may not be such a bad proposition after all.

Of course, keep in mind that you still have other options such as:

- Accepting the unpaid work on the condition that you can take on another job that does pay

- Asking if your work can be reviewed after two weeks to determine if it's worth paying you to continue

- Asking your academic advisor how to get academic credit for the work as an independent study

- Depending on the employer, finding out if you can have free use of the employers' products or services in some way

Note: More options are listed in the "Make Your Own Internship" section under "Select Your Hours and Compensation."

The bottom line is that internships serve to help you gain experience and exposure. They are an investment that forms the basis of a profitable career with the employer or within the industry you are pursuing.

Aim: Targeting Opportunities

- Timing the Search

- Which Track Should I Take?

- Making Your Own Internship

Timing the Search

The timeline of your search may be dependent on which methods are available to you for finding, applying to, and securing internships. Internship deadlines vary in different industries and making your own internship will require different steps (and a potentially longer process) than applying through a formal recruiting program.

Here is a minimum of the stages involved in the process of applying:

- Clarify your goals for obtaining an internship
- Decide what kind of internship you want—projects, industry, time commitment, location
- Determine when you will be available to start your internship
- Find out about existing opportunities or if you will be making your own project/internship
- Put together your application package: resume, cover letter outline, references
- Research industry/organizations and prepare for interviews
- Chart deadlines for the internships of interest—application due dates, when recruiting starts, etc.
- Prioritize your application efforts based on deadlines and how they rank in helping you meet your goals
- Interview, follow-up
- Make back-up plans—does this involve casting a wider net?
- Receive offers, commit to the best choice

Each of the above steps takes some time. If you are unclear about your career goals, you might need longer than if you are focused and know which companies or functional skills you want to target. In general, you should plan several months in advance of when you hope to start your internship.

Which Track Should I Take?

There are several options for identifying and securing internships. Whether you are identifying opportunities and interviewing through on-campus recruiting programs or other methods, understand that you are ultimately your own headhunter. Some things to keep in mind in order to build and maintain this attitude are:

- Determining employers for whom you most want to work
- Making an internship plan using "bridge" employers
- Focusing your message for maximum effect
- Recognizing that an employer is looking for overall fit, not just skills
- Making sure you are *selling* yourself in your interviews and conversations
- Remembering to ask for the job and to close the interview
- If you are turned down by an employer's main office, finding someone at a regional office with whom to discuss opportunities

With this mindset, you will truly have control over your career development. While you certainly want to get as much benefit out of any and all on-campus interview opportunities, do not give up responsibility for your career path to the career office. Keep your options open, and continue to forge ahead.

School Program/On Campus

So what does the on-campus recruiting process look like, and how can you use it to your advantage? Check with your career center for your school's procedures. In general, on-campus recruiting follows a similar pattern to that of the MBA internship recruiting, process described here:

1. You'll start by registering with the career office and completing a profile that includes at least one version of your resume.

2. You will either bid on interview slots or submit a resume to be considered for competitive interview slots.

3. Then, you will complete on-campus interview(s) with employers who have chosen you to be part of their interview line-ups.

4. If all goes well, next-round interviews will take place at select employers' office locations. Throughout the process, a chunk of your time will go toward networking and sending thank-you notes.

At first blush, this on-campus recruiting process seems simple, egalitarian, and efficient. The truth is that it's more often a complex, totalitarian, and cumbersome process. The most qualified candidate isn't the one who will necessarily get the job. Why tell you this? Because, in order to be successful, you'll need to practice working within the system.

Here are some tactics for working effectively within the system:

- Write to the contacts you've made at your five premier and five bridge employer companies who are coming to campus, and let them know of your interest in internship or summer opportunities, regardless of whether they are interviewing for interns with your major or graduate studies focus. If you find that any one of these contacts is not the person to talk to, find out who is.

- If you aren't selected for an interview, write to the contact to ask for an alternative venue through which to express your interest and desire to work with them.

- If you don't hear back from a company contact, show up early at the interview site on the day of the interviews (dressed as if for an interview, with resume at the ready), and ask if you can have two to three minutes of the representative's time.

- If you get a "no" at some point during this process, take it gracefully and abort the process. Still do send the representative a thank-you note and reiterate your interest in interning for the company. Now, maybe you can find another person in the organization (a friend or alum) who can forward your resume internally.

Researching Off-Campus Opportunities

The steps for securing opportunities with employers who do not participate in campus recruiting programs (hence, these are called off-campus employers) follow the same basic pattern as the on-campus process: agree to an opportunity, determine fit, and speculate on the offer. However, going the off-campus route will typically open up a much wider range of ways for landing an internship. If the opportunity were with an employer who has an internship program in place, the path you'd take here would share a strong similarity to the on-campus process. However, in many cases, you'll need to create the opportunity for yourself. This seminar in creative thinking is covered is greater detail in the "Make Your Own Internship" section of this guide.

There are a multitude of resources available to you to identify potential companies or organizations that may be able to offer internships. Often campus career centers provide a database of current internship or summer/short-term opportunities. The following kinds of resources are available, and be sure to check out the "For Your Reference" section at the end of the guide for specific suggestions.

Internet resources. The Internet can be a very productive tool for doing preliminary research on companies and industries. Visit job and internship sites (which often include databases searchable by career field or location); peruse company homepages and human resources pages; get tips from career center websites at local universities, which typically provide a relevant set of resource links and have their own internship databases.

Publications. Many print publications exist that compile lists of existing internship programs. These publications address specific industries, international opportunities, and "top" internships. Many are updated annually and contain contact information and descriptive summaries, including qualifications and deadlines.

Job fairs. Campus and industry job fairs offer a good opportunity to investigate internships. Many campus career centers will post calendar information on upcoming job fairs. You can also check local newspapers and industry publications or association websites for job fair announcements. Go to these job fairs prepared to speak directly with company representatives on current or future opportunities. It helps to have a resume prepared and a focused message to make the most of your and the recruiter's time.

Professional associations. Associations often offer their members a professional development component, and may be able to direct you towards relevant internship and training opportunities. Additionally, networking through professional associations in your field of interest is a good way to make connections and learn the inside scoop on which employers are hiring.

Personal networks. Using your existing social, familial, and professional/peer networks to establish an internship is a great way to get started pursuing opportunities. One former intern, who utilized connections through his peers to land himself an international internship in Hong Kong, attests to this: "You are going to be able to find a wider variety of opportunities more quickly and more individually tailored than you would through a formal channel." After identifying the employer's need, he negotiated a unique role for himself and was hired into a paid internship.

Making Your Own Internship

When you go out to eat, do you prefer to go to restaurants where you can get your food to order (sauce on the side, hold the anchovies, medium rare, etc.), or where you can actually prepare it yourself (salad bars, buffets, select your steak or lobster, build your own sundae, etc.)? If you think about it, how many restaurants *don't* allow you to customize your meal in some way? Can't think of any, can you?

This exercise of customizing something to suit your wants and needs also translates—or should—to your work life. True, many of us have learned to mask or lose sight of our true professional goals and dreams (it's called being stuck in the rat race). But, if given the opportunity, there are any number of things we could come up with if asked, "What would you change in your job if you could?" and/or "What are the elements that make up an ideal job?"

During the course of your career, and during stints with various employers, you will have ample opportunity to work yourself into your dream role. Carrying out a tailored internship, summer project, or volunteer work is just one way to get you there. It carries tremendous potential: Because you have a greater ability and flexibility to mold it into the shape and form you most want, an internship of your own making can get you that much closer to your goal. That said, be sure to not only sell your abilities but also the idea of an internship as a vehicle through which you can add value to the business at hand.

Select Your Functional Area

Selecting the functional area in which you want to work is fundamental to your future career. For example, most MBAs starting B-school are willing to work in a variety of disciplines (finance, marketing, operations, systems, management, etc.). That said, you can't be all things to all people. To make the most impact on potential employers, pick one functional area as your key area of concentration. Without this focus, your message will be loose, your direction vague, your enthusiasm likely diluted. Once you've selected your key area of concentration, your messages are more likely to be tight and targeted, your direction focused, your enthusiasm genuine and strong, and your overall outlook realistic and healthy.

Select Your Industry/Employer

The tactic of creating an internship or summer project can work with almost any employer. The likelihood of being able to create your own project and get paid for it is better with employers who do not already have a formal internship program. However, don't give up on employers with formal internship programs if that's where your interests lie. Many of these existing programs are coordinated from a regional or national headquarters office. These same employers may have branch offices that probably do not take part in their corporate offices' internship program and could just as likely use some additional help during the summer or for particular projects.

Select Your Project

Find someone in the department where you would like to work. Talk with him or her about the projects that are sitting on the shelf gathering dust. Be prepared to discuss some of your project ideas or to at least jumpstart their thinking. Once you start delving into the kind of work they need help with, begin to interject with some of the things you'd like to be doing as well and see if those pieces can be integrated with the work they want done. This way, you are helping solve the employer's problem, while also taloring the project against what you'd like to learn or gain experience in. Having a solid command of the terms or lingo used by the employer and that particular industry will give you a leg up in matching your needs against those of your potential employer's.

If you are making contact with companies who have structured or centralized recruiting groups, be prepared to be directed to recruiting coordinators or campus liaisons in the companies' attempts to shuffle you into their generic recruiting pipeline. If they try to redirect you, tell your contact you want to create a unique experience that wouldn't be available through an internship program and that you prefer to trade some compensation in return for gaining more control over what work you will do. Refer to the "Get over Cold-Calling Cold Feet" worksheet to help you get your foot in the door and to start talking with prospective employers about individualized internships or short-term projects.

Get Over Cold-Calling Cold Feet

The following are sample scripts to help guide you when conducting cold calls for independent internships or summer projects. Use the parts you are comfortable with, and create new scripts for yourself once you have made some calls and gained some confidence.

Motivation—Getting Started

Cold calling is tough; no doubt about it! So make your first five calls to people who are likely to be more receptive. These are people like:

- Friends and family in the working world
- Alumni in jobs at companies you want to work for
- Peers within the program that you can practice with
- Career advisors (get feedback on your approach)
- Friends of peers in the program

Really practice the "[insert name of friend/peer] recommended I talk with you" portion of your calls.

- Be friendly
- Be targeted
- Be concise
- Be sincere
- Be insightful

And you'll get hired!

Aim

Get Over Cold-Calling Cold Feet (cont'd.)

Sample Scripts for Talking with Receptionists/Gatekeepers

Hints. These are folks who have been trained to screen calls and direct job hunters to their website or to an HR or recruiting person. So tell them you would like to speak with someone in the [fill in blank] department to better understand the work they do.

Before your call is transferred, ask for the name of the person with whom you are being connected.

Voice Mail Script. "Hello. My name is [insert your name]. I am a student in the [insert name] program at the School of [insert name] at [insert name] University. I would like to speak to someone in your [insert department name] department to learn more about the type of work they are doing. I will contact you later this week to see whom you would recommend I speak with. If you are able to forward this message to the appropriate person in the [insert department name] department, they can contact me at [insert your phone number]. Thank you!"

Live Script. "Hello. My name is [insert your name]. I am a student in the [insert name] program at the School of [insert name] at [insert name] University. I would like to speak to someone in your [insert department name] department to learn more about the type of work they are doing. Can you transfer me to a manager who oversees work that involves [insert type of work]?

Possible responses and scripts for your reply

"Why?"

"I'm trying to learn more about the [insert type of work] type of work in the [insert industry name] industry. Talking to people who do that work is the best way for me to understand it."

Aim

"No!"

"Could you pass along a message to someone for me then? I'm trying to learn more about the [insert type of work] type of work in the [insert industry name] industry. Talking to people who do that work is the best way for me to understand it."

"Go to our website."

"I've been there [*don't lie!*]. But it doesn't talk about the type of [insert type of work] work that's going on in the [insert department name] department/group. That's why I'd like to chat with someone who's actually doing that type of work. Who would you recommend I talk with?"

"I can't give names."

"I understand the need to protect everyone's privacy. If you know someone who would be good to talk to about the [insert type of work] work within the [insert name of department] department/group, can you transfer me to his or her voice mail so that I can leave a message?"

Hints for Talking with HR Managers/Recruiters/Staffing Personnel

It's difficult to know whether these people are decision-makers (you should talk with them in detail if they are) or paper pushers (these are people who are told what to do).

A good default position is to ask them to direct you to someone who is actually in the job or who oversees the job you are interested in.

Use the scripts for receptionists. If the person you're talking to sounds and acts like a decision-maker, switch over to the scripts for the line managers and ask them about the work itself. If they aren't sure of the actual work being done, ask if you can talk with someone who is doing the work or who oversees the work.

Sample Scripts for Talking with Line Managers/People Doing the Work

Hint. Be respectful of their time, their knowledge, and their ability to connect you to other people.

Voice Mail Script. "Hello. My name is [insert your name]. I am a student in the [insert name] program at the School of [insert name] at [insert name] University. [Insert name] recommended I speak with you. To supplement my studies, I would like to talk with you about the types of work and projects you currently have under-way, and to understand your perspective on the [insert name of industry] industry. As you might imagine, I'm also putting together projects I can do this summer to get hands-on experience in the [insert name] area. One project idea that comes to mind, based on reading about your [fill in blank] work, is [fill in blank]. My interests and training are focused in [fill in blank], and I have [insert number of years] years of experience in [fill in blank]. You can reach me at [insert contact info]. I will be in touch in the next few days and look forward to talking with you soon. Thank you."

Live Script. "Hello. My name is [insert your name]. I am a student in the [insert name] program at the School of [insert name] at [insert name] University. [Insert name] recommended I speak with you. Do you have a few minutes to talk?"

Possible responses and scripts for your reply

"Now is a good time to talk."

"I appreciate the time to talk with you. To supplement my studies, I would like to talk with you about the types of work and projects you currently have under-way, and to understand your perspective on the [insert name of industry] industry. As you might imagine, I'm also putting together projects I can do this summer to get hands-on experience in the [insert name] area. One project idea that comes to mind, based on

Aim

reading about your [fill in blank] work, is [fill in blank]. Can you tell me a little about the main projects you currently have under-way?" [Use some questions from the "Cold-Calling Questions" worksheet that follows.]

"Can't talk now."

"I know you're very busy, which is one of the reasons I'd like to schedule some time to talk with you at a later date. When can we arrange ten minutes or so to talk that would be more convenient for you?"

"What's an internship [or summer project]?"

"A summer project could be almost anything we decide on. Ideally, it would be very meaningful and necessary for you and your department or team, while providing me with some in-depth experience and opportunities to exercise my skills and develop others. For instance, since it appears you are doing [fill in blank], I could assist with [fill in blank] or [fill in blank] in some way. Can we talk more about that?"

"We don't have a budget."

"I understand how tight things must be. I just want to gain some good experience and exposure. What types of projects are in need of attention right now?"

"How much will it cost?"

"We could approach this many different ways:

- "You could pay me, say, $20 to $30 an hour for however many hours I work per week."

- "Perhaps I could work two weeks at $10 to $15 an hour. Then we could re-evaluate the impact of my work and level of pay."

- "I might even be able to work two days a week for free for a month. Then we could re-evaluate things, and talk about a fair amount I could be paid after that."

- "I am mainly looking for an opportunity to learn—perhaps we could talk about the possibility of participating in your organization's conferences or other training activities?"

"There's no work."

"Thank you for being candid. Could we still talk for a moment about the types of projects you have underway? If I can better understand the challenges and opportunities you face, it will help me set my expectations for the present time and for the rest of my academic program."

At the End. "Would you recommend I talk with anyone else there who does [fill in blank] type of work? Or do you know someone at another company doing [fill in blank] type of work who could use a hand over the summer?"

Aim

Cold-Calling Questions

Use this tool once you have a call or meeting scheduled to get more information about a role, group, department, or organization. It is very important to adapt these questions so that they are relevant to the department, project, role, or positions that interest you. Keep these questions in mind, take note of the unique lingo used by your contact, and hit your selling points (transferable skills, experiences, knowledge, etc.). In informational interviewing, it's important to connect with the person. These are some questions to get you started, but remember to use your own words.

About the Org Chart

How does this role (position or department) fit into the larger organization?

Unique Lingo Used:

_____

Your Selling Points:

_____

What is the size of your department/group?

Unique Lingo Used:

_____

Your Selling Points:

_____

How centralized is the group?

Unique Lingo Used:

_____

Your Selling Points:

_____

Cold-Calling Questions (*cont'd.*)

How is information within the organization typically communicated?

Unique Lingo Used:

_____

Your Selling Points:

_____

About the Role/Career

What are some of the current challenges?

Unique Lingo Used:

_____

Your Selling Points:

_____

What profit & loss responsibilities does each team have? [MBA or managerial]

Unique Lingo Used:

_____

Your Selling Points:

_____

Can you describe the (cyclical) nature of the work or department?

Unique Lingo Used:

_____

Your Selling Points:

_____

Cold-Calling Questions (*cont'd.*)

What is the typical length of the main projects?

Unique Lingo Used:

_____

Your Selling Points:

_____

What's the management style like within the company or department?

Unique Lingo Used:

_____

Your Selling Points:

_____

What are the opportunities for growth and promotion?

Unique Lingo Used:

_____

Your Selling Points:

_____

What are some typical last-minute issues?

Unique Lingo Used:

_____

Your Selling Points:

_____

Cold-Calling Questions (*cont'd.*)

About Success Factors

Is this a new role or vacancy?

Unique Lingo Used:

_____

Your Selling Points:

_____

If a vacancy, what did people previously in the role do well, not well?

Unique Lingo Used:

_____

Your Selling Points:

_____

What are some of the key metrics and expectations for the role?

Unique Lingo Used:

_____

Your Selling Points:

_____

What are some critical challenges?

Unique Lingo Used:

_____

Your Selling Points:

_____

Aim

Cold-Calling Questions (*cont'd.*)

Is taking initiative or innovating encouraged?

Unique Lingo Used:

_____

Your Selling Points:

_____

Can you describe the performance review process?

Unique Lingo Used:

_____

Your Selling Points:

_____

How is the volume of work for this role measured?

Unique Lingo Used:

_____

Your Selling Points:

_____

What are the most critical attributes needed to be successful?

Unique Lingo Used:

_____

Your Selling Points:

_____

Select Your Team

When talking with a prospective employer about the projects you can do for them, keep in mind that you're in a good position to also ensure that you work with the appropriate internal people or groups to better gain the exposure and experience you want. To make sure you get to work with such key people, research the company thoroughly and pay close attention to the language and terminology used by your prospective employer when he or she describes the type of work available. Consider mapping out your ideal internship/volunteer or summer project experience. For example:

Functional Area: Finance focus—with some marketing thrown in, if possible

Industry/Employer: Big real estate development and management firms/companies

Project:

1. Develop a model to identify optimum mid-market locations for multi-anchored retail centers

2. Determine how best to promote these opportunities internally and to investors

3. Present the findings to the most senior members of the company as possible

Team: The ideal team would involve:

1. Demographic research

2. Finance

3. Project development

4. Marketing

5. Investor relations

6. Executive review committee

The last portion of your project map lists the people and/or groups you'd like to interact with to accomplish your work. Talking about these points during the planning stages of the project doesn't necessarily guarantee your interaction with them. However, the chances of having these people and groups on your project are more likely if you make them part of the planning early on.

Select Your Hours and Compensation

While established internship programs typically have a standard duration, set of hours, and compensation associated with them, projects that you create and agree upon with an employer are much more flexible and open to negotiation. Expect to be paid less, on average, or to receive no pay at all. Since you probably still have bills to pay, you and the employer may agree to a schedule that has you working less than full-time. Some ways you can structure the hours and pay for the project include:

1. **Working part-time, for free, for the entire internship/project.** Or working full-time without pay, but only for a limited amount of time, say four to six weeks. In either case, if you are planning on a summer project or internship, you have the opportunity to take another job that does pay.

2. **Working full-time for, say, two to four weeks,** and then having a pre-arranged review meeting at which time the employer will decide whether to pay you to complete your work. (You can still choose to complete the project while working elsewhere to earn some more money.)

3. **Agreeing to a flat fee that is then paid in thirds.** One-third upfront. One-third following a pre-determined review during the middle of the project. And the final third upon the successful completion of the project.

4. **Agreeing to a trade.** The employer may have a product or service you can receive in lieu of wages. This may include professional development activities—such as participating in seminars, trainings, and conferences.

Select Your Full-Time Job

If you have successfully created an internship or project customized to your particular strengths and ambitions—and if you're able to make a vital impact on the employer because of it, you are now well positioned to discuss full-time opportunities. It might be that you want a job doing exactly what your project required—and you've just proven to them how successful you would be doing it. Or it may be that you've made strong inroads into other groups or divisions while at the company. If so, you can apply the same methods you used when you secured the original project in order to get a full-time role with these new groups. In either case, the way in which you created and completed the project demonstrates to the employer that you have the desire and follow-through to make tangible impacts on the business.

If you decide not to pursue full-time opportunities with the same employer, you will still reap numerous benefits from your customized project such as:

- Tremendous experience and exposure
- Tangible and transferable skills
- A better sense of what you want to do and with whom
- Good contacts within the industry
- A solid understanding of industry tools, language, and practices

Aim

- Enhanced negotiation skills
- A boost in your self-confidence and self-worth

The most critical elements to come out of a well-orchestrated, customized independent project are the drive and determination needed to find a full-time job that's best for you.

Make Your Own Internship

Use this worksheet to help you create the best independent internship or project experience you can possibly have.

Functional Area: Choose from the functional areas such as accounting, finance, information systems, management, marketing, operations, etc.

One major function: _____

One minor function: _____

Industry/Employer: First, narrow your search to an ideal industry. From there, select specific employers to target.

Industry: _____

Employer: _____

Employer: _____

Employer: _____

Employer: _____

Project: Have specific elements (topics, methods, outcomes, etc.) in mind for your project. Tailor your project suggestions to each employer with whom you talk.

	Your Words	**Their Lingo**
Element:	_____	_____
Element:	_____	_____
Element:	_____	_____
Element:	_____	_____
Element:	_____	_____

Team: Think about which people, groups, teams, divisions, or committees you want your project to involve, and talk about this with the employer upfront, while mapping out the project.

	Your Words	**Their Lingo**
Person/Group:	_____	_____
Person/Group:	_____	_____
Person/Group:	_____	_____
Person/Group:	_____	_____
Person/Group:	_____	_____
Person/Group:	_____	_____

Aim

Get Hired: The Process

- Be the Ideal Candidate

- Getting the "Yes"

- International Students

- Americans Pursuing Internships Abroad

- Refusing to Take "No" as the Final Answer

Be the Ideal Candidate

Several employers responding to NACE's *Job Outlook* 2003 survey offered practical advice to college students about how to become a "perfect job candidate," as follows:

- **Research the company before the interview.** "Each year, employers cite researching the organization as the single most important piece of advice they can offer candidates. There is no substitute for research, so do your homework: Research the company (and the position, if possible) before you interview. This will enable you to ask intelligent questions during the interview."

- **Be open-minded.** "It's extremely important to look at all the factors connected to a job opportunity. Don't let salary alone determine whether you take or nix a job offer; you need to consider the work involved, stability of the company, corporate culture, and work environment. These are more likely to have an impact on your long-term satisfaction and deserve to be given weight."

- **Gain relevant work experience.** "Employers place a lot of emphasis on candidates having relevant work experience even when they are scrambling to find qualified candidates, to say nothing about when there are more top-notch candidates to choose from. Although it's not necessarily a requirement for many opportunities, having relevant work experience gives you a distinct advantage over inexperienced candidates. In addition, you'll be better prepared to make a decision about the type of job and work environment that best suits you. And, there's one other key advantage: Many employers turn first to their own interns and co-op students when they have jobs available."

Note: To find out more about the NACE Job Outlook 2003 survey, go to the resource section at the end of this guide, or visit the NACE website: www.naceweb.org.

In other words, in order for you to be the ideal candidate you need to have a clear and insightful understanding of the organization and industry or career field in which you want to work. You must also understand and be able to articulate your own goals and how they match or compliment those of the organization. Finally, get some experience; building the foundation that demonstrates your skills and accomplishments is the first step towards your next hire.

Companies Screen Out, not In

If you haven't been on an interviewing team for an employer, you may think the interview process holds to a relatively open-door policy, one that focuses on reasons why a candidate should be hired. However, the fact is that the process is geared to screen *out* candidates. Just think of the terminology that's used to describe what takes place during the recruiting process:

- Weeding out or dinging candidates
- Culling through resumes
- Thinning out the prospects
- Screening through the applicants

The recruiting process is after all about selecting the best, not hiring the rest. Your goal then is to portray yourself as the best person for the job. Employers have a multitude of reasons for removing a candidate from consideration for an internship. Here are ten top reasons:

1. A letter that is not addressed to a specific person (e.g., Dear MBA Recruiter, To Whom it May Concern, or ATTN: Vice President, Marketing)

2. A resume that does not have good layout and structure, and/or does not reflect the skills required of the position

3. A letter/interview style that overuses generic phrases like "your company" or "your position" in a way that indicates it is just that—a generic messages being sent to any number of employers

4. Poor communication skills (poor grammar, spelling, speech)

5. Poor preparation

6. Poor grooming/attire

7. Poor manners

8. Lack of enthusiasm

9. No effort made at building rapport

10. Too arrogant or, on the flip side, no self-confidence

Don't lose heart. You can turn all of these points around with the following measures:

1. Find a specific person to whom you can send a letter or with whom you can communicate.

2. Have your resume reviewed and reviewed and reviewed again!

3. Use the employer's name as well as the specific position a couple of times in your letter and during the interview.

4. Practice, practice, practice. You can script out voice mails in advance. Have your letters reviewed (yes, and reviewed again). Conduct a mock interview and videotape it, if possible. Then review the tape and take notes about the things you did well and the areas you'd like to improve.

5. Research an employer. Talk to former employees and interns who are in your school or who've graduated recently. Be thoughtful and articulate about the knowledge you've acquired. Again, practice!

6. Find out what the dress protocol is for an employer from former employees and interns. Be sure to have professional attire ready before the day of the interviews—consider having the career office review your clothes a few days before your interviews if you are unsure.

7. Be conservative. Be sensitive. And be mindful and respectful of the employer's representatives. If you find you have a complaint about an employer, it's best to address it with your career office first, when possible.

8. Review what you look for in an employer and a role. Think about what gets you excited in your work. Recognize that you, indeed, are a great candidate for the position. And figure out how this employer has just what it is you're looking for.

9. Be friendly and conversational, all in a natural manner. Ask diplomatic, clarifying questions in an interview, over the phone, or in your correspondence.

10. Get feedback from your peers about your conversational style. For example, if you come off sounding cocky, work at toning down your delivery. If your delivery is halting and your tone of voice too soft and retiring (i.e., you sound unsure of yourself), then work on achieving a smooth and enthusiastic delivery, recognizing that you have a lot to offer.

Getting the "Yes"

Common sense tells you that when it comes to securing an internship, you should make every effort to conduct yourself in a manner similar to that of your employer. This doesn't mean you should pretend to be something you're not. However, if you go about selecting potential employers based on insightful research, chances are you're going to find a match with an employer who in turn is more likely to find a match in you.

The key word here is *research*. Talk with people who are doing the work you'd like to do. Speak with alumni or personal contacts who have worked or are currently working at your prospective employer's company. Find time with students/peers who had internships in the same functional area and/or industry as the one in which you are interested. Likewise, sit down with students who are ahead of you in your program and have backgrounds similar to yours or are headed in a similar career direction. Overall, the critical element is to gather firsthand data. Sure, you can spend time focused on company websites and industry journals. But you won't get insights into the nuances of an industry or the inner workings of an employer that way.

The Right Lingo

In the previous chapter, getting a handle on the language used in an industry and by an employer was first mentioned as vital to being able to create your own internship or independent project. Likewise, the same is true for any interviews that could lead to a role as part of an established internship program.

Have you ever ordered a meal in an ethnic restaurant that had the native names of the foods written phonetically in English, along with some type of numbering system to help the customers while ordering? You might first try to pronounce the name of the dish you want, or at least hold up the menu to show the server the item you would like, only to have them lean over your shoulder and say, "Oh, you want number 17." In an interview, you must be able to speak intelligently about the role in which you are interested, and to ask questions accordingly, because the interviewer is certainly not going to lean over the table and say, "Oh, you must mean job #7 in department #12." If you can speak the language of the employer and the industry, the recruiter is that much more assured not only of your interest in them, but also of your potential fit with the company.

The Right Questions

It is crucial to understand the scope of business for which you are interviewing. The current hiring supervisor for an undergraduate internship program at a major consulting firm offers the following words of caution to would-be interns: "You can kill yourself with the first question you ask if it is too vague or shows lack of knowledge or research into the company." Company recruiters often share information with each other—once you've made the impression that you are uniformed or uninterested, you will be scrambling to make up for it.

Most of us are familiar with the phrase, "There's no such thing as a stupid question." The caveats to this notion are that, indeed there are stupid questions when 1) first meeting your potential in-laws; and 2) when interviewing for a job. In a nutshell, you should not ask questions during an interview that several minutes on the employer's website could have answered. Some examples of good questions to ask are listed on the "Cold Calling Questions" worksheet in the previous section. Of course, be aware you may have the opportunity to ask just two or three questions, so choose wisely.

The Right Rapport

Pretty much the first question an interviewing group will ask when they get together after talking with a candidate is, "What do you think?" And the first responses to that question are mostly emotional or gut reactions. Eventually, a candidate's responses to questions may be deliberated, but only after a very general pulse has been taken. It's this general pulse that reflects how well the candidate has been able to build a rapport among the individuals with whom he or she has spoken.

By definition, rapport is an emotional bond or friendly relationship between people based on mutual liking, trust, and a sense that they understand and share each other's concerns. Some employers refer to it by calling it "fit." They will ask themselves, "Is this candidate the right fit for the job, for the team, and for us?" What they're driving at is this: "Is this someone I want working for me, with me, or with my clients and customers?"

If you build a strong rapport with one or more members of the recruiting team, they can act as advocates on your behalf during the interviewing teams' deliberations. But how do you establish rapport, let alone build it? Here are ten things that, if done well, will help you establish rapport with your interviewer. They are all based on being friendly and respectful.

1. Be on time.

2. Dress appropriately (professional attire; if you are unsure, err towards conservative).

3. Greet the interviewer warmly (eye contact, smile, friendly handshake).

4. Let the interviewer know upfront that you're glad to have the opportunity to interview.

5. Maintain an attentive, engaging, and enthusiastic demeanor and attitude throughout the interview (i.e., remain calm and responsive). Humor in small doses is also a good thing.

6. When starting to respond to a question, occasionally give a brief overview of the points you want to cover and verify them with the interviewer. For example, "There's a particular project I have in mind when I worked at ABC company that involved aspects of finance, marketing, and operations. If that sounds like an example you're looking for, I can go into some of the details of my work there."

7. When giving responses to questions, occasionally end with a question of your own. For example, "Which of those points can I go into more detail for you?" or "What projects that I just mentioned would you like more information about?"

8. If a question is vague or unclear, ask clarifying questions. This is almost mandatory during case-style interviews.

9. Make sure you "close" the interview. Reiterate your interest in the position, and ask for the interviewer's business card. Get and give a friendly, closing handshake as well.

10. Send a personalized thank-you note within 24 hours. Include thoughtful comments about the interview and a follow-up mention about something personal that the interviewer said: "Good luck shopping for that new van," or "I hope the big surprise birthday party is a success this weekend."

In the end, rapport is very subjective. Is your interview performance judged differently during the beginning of the day, before lunch, right after lunch, at the end of the day? Yes, it probably is. The best thing you can do to establish and build a good rapport with your interviewer is to prepare, practice, and mean what you say. Otherwise you will come off as being insincere, and the interviewers will pick up on it very quickly.

International Students' Challenges

While everyone faces his or her own unique set of challenges during the job or internship search, international students must contend with certain obstacles that are especially unique. In particular, if you are an international student, employers are concerned about:

- Communications skills
- Ability to work within the company culture
- Relevance of overseas experience in the U.S. marketplace
- Rigor of secondary education overseas
- Legal questions regarding ability to work in the United States
- Commitment and potential as a "permanent" employee

International students can address these concerns with the following measures:

- Communication skills

  - Ensure resume and cover letter are well written and grammatically correct.

  - Highlight any English-related education and work environments on resume.

  - Leave well-crafted and scripted voice mails for those with whom you are networking or contacting about a job.

  - Take conversational English courses if necessary.

  - Express all the nuances of your personality and character in English—enthusiasm, candor, humor, curiosity, insight, etc. Your employment chances are greatly improved this way—as opposed to falling back on words and phrases in your native tongue.

- Ability to work within the company culture: Mention any exposure and experience in industries, work environments, and functional areas similar to the ones for which the employer is hiring.

- Relevance of overseas experience in the U.S. marketplace: Explain the context of an overseas employer's business if not immediately obvious to the reader in your resume and cover letter. For example: "Micro Eletrônica—the largest circuit board manufacturer in Brazil."

- Rigor of secondary education overseas: Highlight the stature of the institution and the student's grades and/or graduation rank in your resume and cover letter. For example: "Delhi University (the third-largest engineering university in India) June 1998; Bachelor of Engineering, Class rank 14/367; all courses were taught in English."

- Legal questions regarding ability to work in the United States: If you require sponsorship to work permanently in the United States, there is no need to say so on your resume or cover letter.

Of course, U.S. students with ethnic names can also find themselves faced with questions about work authorization and ability to communicate. If you've had to deal with this kind of scrutiny, you may want to state your U.S. citizenship clearly on your resume or in your cover letter. Leaving a voice mail to follow up on a resume and cover letter is also a wise tactic for these students (and for international students as well) to alleviate potential concerns over communication skills.

International students should make sure they understand very clearly the legal limitations of their work situation in the United States. For instance, visas can be issued to an international student to come to the United States for a full-time MBA program, a one-year dual-degree program, or even a semester-long exchange program. And each visa has different work authorization stipulations placed on them. (More information on the different types of educationally related visas is available at the USA Immigration Service website: www.usais.org/studentvisas.htm.)

Most American universities and colleges have an office that assists international students with a wide range of services, programs, and workshops, including furnishing details on how to use Curricular Practical Training (CPT), which allows international students to work while in the U.S. Optional Practical Training (OPT) is also available to some international students; this allows you to work up to a year in the United States following the completion of U.S.-based academic work.

Many employers treat internships as extended interview sessions with students to see if they will make good full-time employees. If a policy is in place that doesn't allow employers to sponsor international students for permanent work authorization, then it goes without saying that they're unlikely to hire international students as interns. That said, there's still a good number of employers who do take international students on as interns and/or will sponsor them for permanent work authorization. Try checking with your career services office to find out which companies do.

Remember that recognizing challenges early is the first step to diminishing any potential limiting effects they may have. Also keep in mind that the advice and steps spelled out in this guide can be used regardless of nationality or work authorization.

Americans Pursuing Opportunities Abroad

Just as with an internship at home, you'll make the most out of your internship abroad if it includes targeted projects that assist you in your career goals. There are many opportunities for students in particular to gain short-term internship experiences or work abroad. These programs are becoming more prevalent as alternatives to traditional study abroad. Additionally, for people who are not affiliated with academic programs, volunteering through structured "service-learning" programs can offer the same benefits as formalized internships.

Develop your sense of focus: Do you want to work in development, educational programs (e.g., teaching English) or in business? Do you want to use or develop language skills? Will you do anything if it gets you an internship in Paris or Singapore? Mapping out your priorities will help you target your search for international opportunities. Take this advice for finding an international internship, from a former intern who successfully found and completed an internship in Hong Kong: "Start broad in focus, and the more you increase your focus, the more you increase your chances of success. It's an iterative process. Keep telling people what you are after." After checking out the resource list at the end of this guide, you'll see exactly the breadth of options available to you. As you explore these possibilities, tighten your focus and your message; this will make clear to potential employers how your skills and interests match their needs.

Work Permits/Visas for Students

A work permit for a paid internship (or short-term employment) in most countries must be obtained before heading abroad. The Council on International Educational Exchange and BUNAC are two major organizations that grant students or recent graduates with a work permit, for a fee. These organizations provide authorizations for different countries; check with their websites to determine which will suit your internship goals. U.S.-based formalized programs offering international work exchanges or structured volunteer positions will typically take care of providing their participants with the appropriate papers to work in the placements they offer.

American Companies Abroad

You may be interested in working abroad, but for an American company or organization. If you do not already have a work permit for the countries you are considering (i.e., though dual citizenship or other means), this may be one of the easier routes to take. Contact the U.S. offices and find out about opportunities overseas. Conversely, to jumpstart your international career, you may want to target foreign companies with offices in the United States.

Cultural Appropriateness

Be conscious of the fact that foreign institutions may not conduct their hiring processes in the same way as you are accustomed to in the States. For example they may request a CV (or curriculum vitae) instead of a resume, have different ideas of what is appropriate interview and business etiquette, and the like. While it may seem like a given to have relevant language skills to perform well in the international placements which interest you, be sure you are also familiar with the customs and the industry in the country you are targeting. Being able to demonstrate cultural competence is very important for landing the internship, and essential for successfully completing it.

Refusing to Take "No" as the Final Answer

Get Hired

Here's a news flash: When your application is rejected for an on-campus interview opportunity, does that close the book on your chances of getting an internship with that employer? Absolutely not! Remember, the recruiting process, whether for internships or full-time jobs, is about picking a few people to interview from a large pool of applicants. Employers recognize their process for screening and culling prospects isn't perfect. More often than not, employers are willing to give a second look at a candidate who is looking to be reconsidered.

Turn a "No" into a "Maybe"

The odds of turning a "no" into a "maybe" are best when candidates are being considered for the first round of interviews. During subsequent rounds, the odds get leaner. If the employer in question is one of your top-five choices, then it's worth taking the extra time and energy to try to stay in the candidate pool. In a nutshell, you should contact the employer, sell yourself into the role, and request a chance for an interview. If you already know the recruiter, contact him or her. If you know someone from the functional team with whom the intern will work, contact that person. Be straightforward—simple messages always work best. Certainly don't blame anyone other than yourself for not having been initially selected.

If you're given a chance to state your case and are rejected a second time, it's best not to belabor your appeal with the official internship team for two main reasons, both of which could damage your chances for full-time interviews in the future: You don't want to appear high-maintenance, and you don't want to appear to be stalking the company.

If you never get a clear response to your request to be reconsidered for an on-campus interview, your next best move is to show up, dressed appropriately, at the on-campus interview location the day of the interviews. Arrive about 30 minutes before the first interview, and ask to speak with the one of the employer's representatives. Have your resume in a portfolio, ready to hand over. You might get penciled into an open interview slot. But you should also be prepared that your moment to shine may only amount to about two minutes with an interviewer in the hallway. At this point, you just want to be heard, so make the most out of whatever time you get. If the employer cannot talk with you any time that day, find out if you can contact the representative about a phone screen/interview. See the "Scripts to Go from 'No' to 'Maybe'" worksheet for some suggestions on what to say.

If you are come up against a second "no" in the recruiting process, cease and desist. As much as you might like one, the employer does not owe you a detailed explanation about the decision to remove you from the candidate pool. Once your on-campus appeal has been denied, your next best option is to find an off-campus side window to slip through now that the on-campus front door has been closed. For example, if you've been turned down twice by the employer's main office, find a contact in a regional office who might need your help for the summer. Again, going this far is only worth it if the employer in question is one of your top choices.

Off-Campus Interviews and "Maybes"

Most of the tactics mentioned here also apply to off-campus employers with whom you are in touch. The critical difference is that the employers who do not have a structured internship program take longer to make an employment decision than an employer with a formal program. This means that you need to have patience and persistence when dealing with them. The best thing for you to do in regard to your top choice employers is to stay in touch with your key contacts there. When you do touch base, don't just say, "Hi. Just getting back in touch to let you know I'm still looking for an internship or summer project. I would really appreciate anything you can do to help." Give them ideas of projects you could work on, update them on your current work or academic projects, and/or send them a link to a relevant website or other resource they might consider to be of interest.

Scripts to Go from "No" to "Maybe"

Use this worksheet to help create the messages you will use to move your candidacy for a job from "No" to "Maybe." Do not use these scripts verbatim; rather, use them to better craft messages that are tailored to your specific needs and conditions.

Restating your case in a letter or an e-mail to . . .

A. Someone with whom you have not previously met or communicated

Dear Mr./Ms. [insert employer contact's last name]:

During the past few years, my career focus has centered around building skills in _____, _____, and _____ [ideally, these are skills required for the position]. At the same time, I have learned that the environments that draw out my best efforts involve a mix of _____, _____, and _____ [types of challenges, work teams, opportunities, impacts, etc.]. As I prepared for my internship search, spoke with former interns and current employees of [name of the employer, and division, group, practice area as appropriate], and set goals for my ongoing career, the _____ position seemed to be a near exact match between my aspirations and your organizations' needs. So you can imagine my disappointment upon learning I was not selected for an interview.

I wonder if there is any way my application for an interview can be reconsidered. I would happily make myself available at any time you choose to talk about my background and desire to work with [employer's name] this coming summer, either over the phone or during your time on campus.

My resume is attached/enclosed. Perhaps it did not declare clearly enough what I have tried to express in this note. If given the opportunity to interview for the _____ position, I'm confident you will not be disappointed.

I will remain in touch and look forward to hearing from you.

Sincerely,

[Insert your name]

B. Someone with whom you have previously met or communicated

Dear _____ [either a formal greeting as above, or use a first name—choose appropriately]:

When we last spoke at/during [the event or occasion during which you last spoke with this person], I was very grateful for your insight and guidance about _____ and _____. After our conversation, I felt very encouraged about my fit for [employer's name]'s [name of the position] position. So you can imagine my disappointment upon learning I was not selected for an interview.

As I prepared for my internship search, my career focus has centered around building skills in _____, _____, and _____ [skills required for the position]. And I seek out environments that involve a mix of _____, _____, and _____ [types of challenges, work teams, opportunities, impacts, etc.] to bring out my best efforts. Through my research and conversations about [employer's name], a match seemed likely. Our conversation helped confirm that for me.

I wonder if there is any way to have my application reconsidered. Of course, I would happily make myself available, at your convenience, over the phone [or during your time on campus], to talk about my background and desire to work as a [name of position] this coming summer.

My resume is attached/enclosed. Perhaps it, and I, did not clearly express what I have now tried to bring out in this note. If given the opportunity to interview for the [name of position] position, I'm confident you will not be disappointed.

I will remain in touch and look forward to hearing from you.

Sincerely,

[Insert your name]

On the day of on-campus interviews, getting time with the interviewer by talking to . . .

A. Someone in the career office

"Hi. I would like to talk with [employer's name] about the [name of position] position that they are interviewing for today. Though I wasn't selected for an interview, they are one of my top choices. I believe the resume I submitted didn't adequately describe my skills and experience. Is there any way I can get just a moment with the interviewer who is here today? I did write to them, but didn't get a reply. Can I talk with them very briefly before they start their interviews? I would be grateful for any time at all."

B. Someone with the employer, though not one of the interviewers

"Good morning. Who would you recommend I speak to about being considered for the [name of position] position? As it turns out, I don't believe my resume adequately highlighted my skills and experience when I first applied for an interview. Who could I get a moment with to restate what I see as a good match between [employer's name]'s needs and my aspirations and abilities? I would be grateful for any time at all."

C. A recruiter or other decision-maker

"Hello. I really appreciate you taking a moment with me. While I was not initially selected for an interview with you for the [name of position] position today, I feel there is good fit between [employer's name]'s needs and my aspirations and abilities. I wanted to get some time with you to talk more about that. Would you have time to talk with me later today, or can I talk with you for a moment now?"

Scripts to Go from "No" to "Maybe" (*cont'd.*)

Directing a request for phone screen later (if no time's available the day of the interviews) to . . .

A. Someone with the employer, though not one of the interviewers

"I would really like to talk with one of the interviewers at a later time since their schedule is full today. How could I best get in touch with them to arrange a conversation? And can I leave you a note and a copy of my resume for you to hand over to them later?" [Give him or her a resume, write a note for the interviewer, and leave both with the other employer representative to hand to the interviewer later.]

B. A recruiter or other decision-maker

"If no time is available to talk today, when is a good time to reach you to talk over the phone? Though I wasn't selected initially, I'd like a chance to be considered for the role because I strongly feel there is a good fit between [employer's name]'s [name of position] position and my skills and career goals. When would a better time be to talk more about this?"

Stay Hired: Turn Your Internship into a Job

- Make the Most of Your Internship

- Start Working Before You Start Working

- Maximize Your Internship Outcomes

Make the Most of Your Internship

Once you've secured your desired internship or summer project, the majority of your work is still ahead of you. It's during the internship or summer project itself that you establish yourself as a viable candidate for a full-time position. Imagine the interviews preceding the internship as getting you in the door. Now your time at the company through the summer will serve an extended series of interviews. After all, summer projects (internships or otherwise) serve one main purpose: to give you experience and exposure—experience in an area in which you'd like to have a full-time job, and exposure to a company and/or industry in which you would like to secure that full-time job.

That said, your goals for the internship should be to showcase how valuable you can be to your future employer (the one you are working for, or the one you want to work for); and to learn more about the people and the work in the company/industry in which you want a full-time position.

Start Working Before You Start Working

Chances are you did a good deal of research to get you through your interviews and into your internship. You probably learned a bit about the employer and the industry. And you may have even spoken to some former interns and employees. If so, terrific! Be sure to build on this by continuing to learn more about your employer, the industry, and the work you might be doing before your summer job begins.

Since each industry has a language all its own, familiarize yourself with it. If you've ever traveled to a foreign country, you've probably seen (or been part of) interactions between tourists and locals. The overwhelming response to a tourist's attempt to speak in the local language is almost always positive and encouraging. Likewise, you want your internship employer to recognize your use of the language of its industry and organization as a positive and encouraging sign of your interest and familiarity with the company and the work at hand. For career changers moving into unfamiliar functions—for example, from general management to operations, or from a military role into IT—there is also a need to develop language and communication skills that relate to their new career function.

Some places are better than others for learning the company and industry lingo. Target the resources listed below to effectively and efficiently bring yourself up to speed:

- Employer websites, publications, and white papers
- Competitor websites, publications, and white papers
- Industry-related websites, associations, journals, and newsletters
- Functionally related websites, associations, journals, and newsletters

Also, before you begin your internship, talk with people who are going to be on your team. Ask about their careers and professional interests, ongoing projects, challenges, and advice. This will give you a head start toward building a rapport with your team members. You might even be able find out if there is any work you can begin doing in preparation for your internship. These steps should certainly expose you to the language, people, and projects of the employer. They can also serve to show your workmates and supervisors that you are interested, diligent, and enthusiastic about them, their work, and the company as a whole.

You might also consider finding out what other interns will be in your functional area and contact them. Also, if your employer doesn't have many events planned to allow their interns or summer hires to interact with each other, you will have already established a link with them and can more easily get them together during the summer to discuss their projects and goals. Another group that may prove to be a great resource are interns from the previous year. They may supply insight and information that can help you get off to a better start and avoid common or hidden pitfalls.

When you are going into a structured internship, you should also see if you can plant some ideas in the minds of supervisors about the experience and exposure you hope to gain during the summer. Though an internship has a high degree of pre-determined process and structure, there is some amount of flexibility that you will want to leverage as far in advance as possible. For instance, your marketing internship may be with a specific product or service group. You may still be able to influence whether your summer is spent gaining experience and exposure to couponing and pricing strategies and tactics for an existing offering, or to researching, planning, and structuring new offerings. Either of these focuses during a marketing internship could be valuable, but one may be closer to what you actually want to do after you graduate. If so, then talk about it with the appropriate people before you start, in order to ensure you get the experience and exposure you want most.

☑ Checklist: The Work Before Work Begins

Use this checklist to help you complete some important tasks prior to starting your internship or summer project.

☐ Learn about the language of the employer, the industry, and your functional area.

☐ Make contact with current employees of your internship employer.

☐ Locate and talk with other interns who will work for your summer employer.

☐ Talk with MBAs who worked with your internship employer during the previous year.

☐ Discuss project ideas with your internship supervisor and colleagues.

Maximize Your Internship Outcomes

Here are some suggestions for getting the greatest value out of your internship experience, no matter the industry or organization. After all, you worked pretty hard to get to this stage. Be sure to consider the following as you move through your internship or independent project. In the MBA section to follow, you may find more tips that you can apply to your internship to make the most of the experience (see "Internship Timeline for MBAs").

In the Beginning . . .

Learn your way around the organization and familiarize yourself with day-to-day operations. Learn the organizational and departmental structure; read company literature including e-mails, and employee newsletters; introduce yourself to supervisors, coworkers, and peers.

Understand the systems for communication, including the technology. If you are unfamiliar with computer programs or other tools and methods, be sure to take the time to study or ask questions, so that your integration the office operations is smooth. Additionally, learn office protocol for communication—how are meetings conducted, how else is information shared?

Keep in mind the initial objectives and goals you set out for yourself. Begin a record of your activities and accomplishments—this will help you evaluate your experience and stay on track. Check in with your supervisor to get a sense of how meetings and evaluation of your work will occur.

Establishing Rapport/Integrating

A current internship supervisor with a large consulting company makes the following crucial points for interns to integrate themselves smoothly with their new employer: "Understand how your skills and background can support the team. Get yourself into a contributing role after looking at what everyone else is doing on the projects. Stay flexible on assignments, open to the content. And let them find a way to sell you to clients." You come to the internship with your own set of skills and talents. It's up to you to utilize them so that you maximize the contributions that you are making, and the value you are adding to your employer.

Be sure to take the time to speak with your coworkers, supervisors, and peers. Make connections, manage every interaction you have. As you build relations with clients, and your coworkers, remember that each interaction is a two-way assessment. You are demonstrating your professionalism and abilities. At the same time, you should always keep in mind that this is your chance to see how you fit with the organization. As one internship supervisor puts it, your internship gives you the opportunity to find out "if the firm truly lives their values." Every organization or company has values they pitch, such as a balanced lifestyle, encouraging employee input, or being innovative or cutting edge. Are the qualities that attracted you to this employer really in effect? How do you function in the work environment; does it compliment your work style and goals?

Going Above and Beyond

As your internship progresses, get exposure to as many aspects of the organization or department as you can. Take some risks and remember that self-management is also very important: Be sure to stay on top of your projects and express your enthusiasm and interest for your work. The best way to position yourself for future opportunities is to think about what you would do if you returned to the company. Then, begin discussing your goals and researching the hiring process.

Evaluations, Performance Reviews, and Closure

At the end of the internship, you have an opportunity to evaluate your experiences and also provide feedback to your employer, so that the internship program and future interns may benefit. If you have an exit interview, be open and honest about your experience as an intern; focus on the positives and constructive suggestions (you don't want to burn bridges). Listen carefully and with an open mind when you are evaluated. Be prepared to hear about your strengths and areas in which you might improve. This feedback will help you identify where you can learn or change, and sell yourself based on growth in these areas the next time around. Finally, references from your experience and the contacts you have established may be important in helping you land the next work opportunity.

After the Internship

Stay in touch with your internship contacts. Send thank-you notes immediately afterwards to the key people who influenced your experience. Plan to stay in touch with regard to your career or academic progress. Maintaining these relations is a surefire way to know when new job opportunities develop within the organization. You may wish to mentor incoming interns in the program you finished. This is both an opportunity to give back and also maintain or re-establish contacts with your former internship employer.

Special Section for MBAs

- Improving Your Career Options

- The MBA Career-Changer Honeymoon

- Internship vs. Summer Project

- Internship Timeline for MBAs

- Options Outside of Internships

Improving Your Career Options

If you are an MBA student or graduate, you probably view getting an MBA as a true investment in knowledge, in yourself, and in your future career. If so, consider this: Focus leads to experience . . . leads to credibility . . . leads to offers. This should be your mantra as you go about augmenting—and taking advantage of—your MBA degree by finding or creating your ideal internship (i.e., finding your focus), then leveraging the experience and exposure you've gained from that internship into the career you most desire.

According to surveys conducted by the Graduate Management Admissions Council (GMAC), the group that administers the GMAT, more than half of MBA students are looking to improve their career options. In most cases, this means they want to change their careers in some measurable way. Compare this to 70 percent of employers who say they recruit MBAs because they're interested in the experience and applicable skills they possess (for more survey details, check out www.GMAC.org). Does this mean MBAs will be unable to gain new experiences and skills because employers want to hire them for what they already know and can do? No, not at all. What employers are really looking for can be better defined as "transferable"—not exact—skills. Can a banker's skills transfer into a corporate finance role? Sure. Can an ESL teacher's lesson planning, and individual and group intervention skills transfer into a management consulting role? You bet. And a meaningful internship for these two candidates will emphasize their transferable skills, making them even stronger candidates in the eyes of their future employers.

These two career examples beg the question, "How big is the gap between where your career has been and where you want it to go?" Is the gap small enough to hop across, do you need a substantial bridge to cross it, or is it the Grand Canyon of career changes? The broader the gap, the more in need you are of a substantial internship that will help you gain the experience and exposure for which employers are recruiting.

The MBA Career-Changer Honeymoon

Getting accepted into and then starting an MBA program can give you some "free passes" in an employer's eyes. In a way, like honeymooners caught up in the pomp and circumstance of their nuptials and newly wedded state, an employer can become smitten with the pomp and circumstance of an MBA program and the potential of the students within that particular program. In general, employers have high hopes and expectations for what MBAs can accomplish. After all, you must have strong skills and standout qualities to have been accepted into an MBA program, right? With this in mind, employers tend to be open to the fact that many MBAs are career changers. They will, in fact, use these career-changing MBAs to their advantage, bringing new life, alternative perspectives, and renewed vigor into their organizations. This is what can be called the career-changer honeymoon—the window of opportunity in which MBA job seekers can take advantage of employers' open-mindedness and eagerness to hire MBAs in order to catapult themselves into new situations and careers.

An MBA can dramatically increase the odds of a person with a liberal arts degree and no business experience of receiving an offer for a highly competitive business analyst internship by the simple fact that he or she is buoyed by the stature as well as the knowledge imparted by his or her MBA program. As the following table indicates, being in a graduate B-school can help people make distinct changes in their careers. It compares the jobs held by 15 people prior to starting an MBA program with the summer internships they received while in that program. The degree to which people are able to change the direction of their careers even after just one year supports the idea of the career-changer honeymoon.

Examples of MBA Career Changers from May '02 and May '03 Grads

Former			Summer/Intern		
Function	**Title**	**Industry**	**Function**	**Title**	**Industry**
Administration	Fifth-grade teacher	Education	Finance	Summer associate	Investment banking
Operations	System planning engineer	Utilities	Finance	Investment intern	Retirement ass'n
Marketing	Sr. sales rep	Oil & gas	Finance	Finance & operations consultant	Pharmaceuticals
Administration	Sr. comp. specialist	Clothing retail	Information mgmt	Consumer insights intern	Consumer packaged goods
Administration	Asst. vice president	Private investments	Information mgmt	MBA intern	Gaming software
Operations	Performance engineer	Aircraft	Information mgmt	Supply chain IT intern	Grocery retail
Management	Owner/director & producer	Entertainment	Management	Business dev. intern	Medical devices
Operations	Project engineer	Construction	Management	Business analyst	Oil field services
Administration	English teacher	Education	Management	Worldwide business commercial intern	Consulting
Administration	Equal employment advisor	Legal	Marketing	Marketing intern	Pharmaceuticals
Management	Online media director	Advertising	Marketing	eBusiness associate	Financial services
Management	Director, mktg & membership	Nonprofit	Marketing	Category mgmt intern	Consumer packaged goods
Management	Transportation engineer	Design & construction	Operations	Internal consultant	Computers
Management	HR manager	Appliances	Operations	Business operations analyst	Health care
Management	Technical sec'y in gov. commission	Gov't–transportation	Operations	Supply chain analyst	Medical devices

Source: McCombs School of Business (University of Texas, Austin)

MBA employers often display a greater willingness to consider MBA candidates due to the fact that, along with their academic training, these students are more likely to demonstrate focus, clarity, and passion. Keep in mind that you can enhance the honeymoon-like quality of your MBA by giving evidence of your strong direction through student group membership and involvement, course projects, academic practicums, independent studies, and not-for-credit research projects. Together, they can strongly influence a potential employer about the seriousness of your desire for and ability to take on a new career.

Internship vs. Summer Project

Let's divide MBA employers into two camps: those with formal internship programs and those without. Does it matter which camp you take part in during the summer? No. It all looks the same on your resume when everything's said and done. So why even point out the distinction? Because your tactics and message will differ depending on whether the employer has an established MBA internship program.

Internships

In its most typical form, internships are structured programs managed from an employer's headquarters or one of its divisions or regional offices. It's more often the Fortune 500, or the larger of the nonprofit groups, institutions, governmental bodies, private foundations, and associations that have internship programs. Some exceptions include smaller organizations that are within an easy commute of a B-school. Formal internship programs are often a strategic exercise by the employer to find and retain new talent. That said, employers often value MBA interns differently than other new employees; a higher value—along with a higher set of expectations—is often placed on them, such that MBAs typically receive higher levels of compensation in return.

Internships normally span eight to 12 weeks from mid-May to early September, depending on the student's academic calendar. Interns are usually hired into a specific group or division within the employer company. Often they will not know the nature of their first assignment or project until a few weeks before the internship begins. In some cases, they may not get their first assignment until the second week or so of the internship. During the course of their work, interns may be given the opportunity to take part in social gatherings with other interns, key management, and previous interns who are now full-time employees—these are key opportunities for networking. Some employers may also arrange educational lectures and panels, lunches with key executives, and tours of various departments and facilities. In addition to a pay rate that is equivalent to a new MBA's salary, MBA interns may also receive a travel allowance and housing assistance for the summer.

In terms of the work involved, interns are usually assigned to take on a portion of an employer's existing and ongoing work. These assignments are created with key deliverables and milestones set up so that managers can review performance and completed work at least once if not twice during the summer. An internship often culminates with a presentation by the intern to key members of the group or division in which the intern worked. It's not uncommon for senior corporate executives to attend.

Formal internship programs adhere to a strict schedule of application, interview, follow-up and acceptance deadlines. Applications for internships are managed by a specific group or person.

Summer Projects

It makes sense that employers who come to campus looking for MBA interns have some type of internship program in place. If you're dealing with off-campus employers, however, you'll first need to determine if they are in the habit of hiring MBAs for the summer (don't use the term *internship* with them yet). If they are not used to or have no experience hiring MBAs for the summer, don't try to educate them on what an internship is. The words *MBA* and *internship* may translate into an avalanche of process, structure, support, and overhead that can overwhelm and intimidate the prospective employer, who just does n't have the time and energy to get stuck with another drain on their busy schedules. The first impression you make on a potential summer employer should not overwhelm and intimidate!

This is where the words *summer project* come into play. While a potential employer may not know exactly what you mean, he or she can at least understand that you are talking about taking on a project (of some kind) during the summer. In comparison to the possibly overwhelming and intimidating impression made on the employer by using the word *internship*, *summer project* sounds manageable and familiar. In the end, you may come up with a structure that mirrors a formal internship. Or your summer project may remain loosely defined and informal—just so long as both you and the employer are comfortable with what's involved.

Summer projects have a higher tendency to come with low or no pay. Even though the employer realizes some benefits from your work, he or she may just not have the budget to pay you well, or to pay you at all—hence the (probable) reason why no formal internship exists in the first place. The counterbalance to lower pay (or no pay) is that you have created a summer project that's much more tailored to your specific needs than a conventional internship could have been.

Internship Timeline for MBAs

Establish Rapport (Weeks 1 to 2)

The first couple of weeks of your summer work is the time for establishing a solid rapport between you and the people with whom you are working. The three areas you should be most attentive to during this period are: people, methods and tools, and meetings.

People

The people with whom you will work will play a key role in your success during the summer and beyond. That said, here are some specific areas to pay close attention to during your first weeks on the job.

- Learn about the organizational structure of the team, group, department, and division in which you are working. This will help you figure out who the key stakeholders are in the organization, and which ones are using the work you and your group are doing.

- Ask and learn about the key strengths of members within your group. This way you will be better able to ask questions effectively (and to the right person) and get the information you need quickly and easily.

- Find out who in your group or department has made career moves that are similar to your own, and share some stories with them. You never know what useful piece of career advice or insight is just a friendly question away. One question that almost always reveals a nugget or two of useful wisdom is, "In your opinion, what are the most critical two or three pieces of advice for someone new to this group?"

- Take it as fact that the office staff members are extremely influential and have often been in their roles longer than the executives have been in theirs. Members of the office staff include receptionists, mail handlers, assistants and secretaries, runners, office managers, and personnel in the human resources, training and development, technology support, and internal finance and accounting offices, to name just a few. You should respect the impact they have on your ability to complete your work, to navigate the company's systems and policies, to gain access to resources, and to get things done without making a fool of yourself.

Methods and Tools

Find out and become familiar with the core methods and tools that are used by your work group. The quicker you are at mastering them, the sooner you will be able to truly act like a member of the group. Keep in mind, too, that just as employers and their internal groups have their own language, the methods and tools they use contain another layer of language that you will need to learn as well.

- Make sure you are added to the employer's e-mail, voice mail, and inner office mail networks as quickly as possible. Usually, this is arranged prior to your arrival, but don't be surprised if getting a space set up to work in and getting connected are your first projects of the summer. These are also items you can discuss in advance to ensure precious time in your first week isn't spent looking for a cubicle and getting e-mail access, a phone number, and an internal mail routing number.

- Find out what key work methods are used in your group. Does your group use a specific type of software, planning tools, work methodology, or group dynamic process to facilitate the work involved? If so, you will want to know about them early on and get up to speed on them quickly.

- Depending on the types of deliverables that your group typically creates, find out where past examples of the work are stored and how to gain access to them. You will likely have some down time during your first week. Use the time to study the types of deliverables the group has recently produced.

- Find out about the working style of the group. Does it use a meeting management software like Outlook? Or maybe an instant messenger tool like Yahoo! Messenger? It may be that the group works mostly through e-mail or voice mail, or via cell phones or text pagers.

Meetings

Newcomers to an organization often make their first major *faux pas* during a meeting of some kind. That's why it's important to talk about meeting protocols as well as the impact they can have during the first couple weeks of your summer work. Meetings come in all shapes and sizes: daily team meetings, group program reports, project reviews, departmental planning meetings, issues resolution sessions, performance reviews, brain storming sessions, update reports, and more. Some key meeting components that you should be aware of are:

- **Speaking out/talking.** It's very natural for a Type-A MBA personality to use a meeting as a means to showcase his or her ideas, questions, concerns, proposals, rants, criticisms, and objections. You need to recognize that the regularly scheduled meetings in which you are now taking part have unwritten rules of order. If you speak out during the first one or two meetings you attend, you may be perceived to be speaking out of turn. You also might find yourself uninvited from future meetings. It really depends on what expectations exist in the company you're interning with. That said, you are much better off by: 1) asking a trustworthy group member, or your supervisor, about what your expected level of involvement and participation is (and then erring on the side of conservatism); and 2) either in advance or after the meeting, mentioning whatever you would consider saying during the meeting to a trustworthy group member or your supervisor. Once your input has become more regular and appreciated outside of meetings, you can consider being more vocal in the meetings.

- **Etiquette**. The nuances of how a meeting operates can fluctuate depending on the person directing it, and the audience and the technology involved. Be diligent in observing meeting etiquette, and if you participate, take a conservative approach. For instance, if three of your group members are talking at once during a teleconference, avoid speaking since it will only add to the noise in the room and over the phone line. You are much better off taking lessons from the most successfully run meetings and mimicking the behavior you observe there.

- **Your own meetings.** During your summer work, you are probably going to need to arrange some meetings of your own. Discuss them with your supervisor and group members in advance to get their input and ideas.

  - Arrange a meeting or two during the first two weeks of work to clearly define in writing your project schedule and the review, report, and/or presentation periods at the end of your project(s).

  - During your ongoing work, set up meetings with key stakeholders and team members to keep the project moving forward in a timely manner.

  - If your employer does not arrange meetings among summer MBAs, then take the initiative and arrange them.

  - Likewise, you should be thinking about which individuals within the company you want to meet with about your summer work and career goals (more on this type of meeting is covered in the "Build Bridges" section).

Make Connections (Weeks 3 to 4)

By this time, you should know enough to begin feeling comfortable and start settling in. Your projects are underway, and you're ready to make good progress. You should be using terms and tools that now feel more familiar to you and also allow you to make connections between you and your new colleagues. You've identified the folks who can help you—you want to leverage their knowledge while sharing your findings with them. During this two-week period of making connections, keep these points in mind:

- Establish at least two mentors—one who is a peer, and one who is junior to you (a staff member or a person in your group that is younger or at a level lower than yours). You want to create a set of relationships to deepen your knowledge of the group and the company while also having at least two people with whom you can continue to share ideas. Ideally, these mentors each have strong internal and external networks of their own and are people with whom you get along well. Set up a routine time to meet with them before, during, or after work.

- If your ideas and comments are gaining acceptance outside of meetings, begin to mention them during the meetings now. If you attend meetings where no people at your level speak out, ask your supervisor to raise your idea during the meeting, and then let them be the judge of whether it's worth mentioning.

- Establish a list of people in your group and other groups that you'd like to meet with and talk to (see the following checklist, "Get in Touch with the Following People"). Reach out to people at your level, or lower, to talk about their roles and the challenges they face. Find out more about the company in order to make a better, more informed decision about whether you want to have a full-time job there—and, if so, in which group. You might also uncover a great project idea to work on during the summer or later on, once you return to your MBA program (more on this in "Back at B-School").

- If you are not doing the work you were expecting to do, let your supervisor know and make suggestions accordingly. It might be that the plans the two of you discussed during your first two weeks are slow in coming to fruition. Or it could be that the group's business needs changed, and your expertise is needed for some other vital project. In either case, be diplomatic and ask how you might be able to do some of the work the two of you had initially discussed.

- You may find a more interesting project to work on instead of the work you initially discussed with your supervisor. Rather than seeming wishy-washy and asking to change the focus of your work, establish a plan for completing your current work and moving on to the new, more interesting project. Or explain why working on this new project is more impactful and helpful to the company and group than the one on which you are currently working.

| ☑ | **Checklist: Get in Touch with the Following People** |

Use this checklist to prompt you to find and reach out to the following people while at your summer internship.

❏ Other MBA interns working for the summer at the same company.

❏ Former MBA interns who are now full-time employees.

❏ Current employees who made career changes similar to the one you are making..

❏ People, at your level or below, who are in groups that are doing work you might be interested in doing as well.

❏ Staff members who are experts using the tools or technology within the group and employer.

Build Bridges (Weeks 5 to 8)

By weeks five to eight, you will be running at full steam—driving things forward with regular status meetings, preliminary drafts, and intermediate releases of your findings in order to better gauge where your project should evolve before you wrap it up. That said, let's talk about the more subtle aspects of these middle weeks—the relationships you have with various people and how you are using them to build bridges for your career.

• Make sure that the mid-summer review you arranged during your first week actually takes place. The review should focus on your performance and impact as well as ways you can improve. This accomplishes a number of goals, the most important of which include: getting across that your performance and the impact of your work are important to you; finding out how to improve your work in order to increase its impact on the group and your summer employer; learning how to improve your working style and "fit" within the group and employer; and confirming the final review and presentation meetings at the end of your stint.

- Use breakfasts and lunches with your newly found mentors and contacts to network and expand your knowledge. Continue to find out about how the work you and your group is doing impacts other parts of the organization. Keep your eyes open for new project ideas, and share them among your contacts. After all, you can't do all the work yourself. And your contacts may appreciate good ideas that they can take back to their groups.

- Reach out to people whom your mentors, group members, contacts, and supervisors have told you about. Find out if you can arrange information-gathering calls to learn about their organizations and their industry perspective. During these calls, you could also find out about projects they are doing and ones they have put on hold. If they are employers you would like to work for full-time, this project information could become very valuable to you (more on leveraging this project information is covered later in the "Options without Internships" section).

- If you are interested in full-time opportunities with your summer employer, find out from your supervisor, the recruiting and human resources team, and other appropriate contacts about their outlook on full-time positions. Ask them, "What can I do to ensure I am a strong candidate for any full-time positions in the ABC group?"

- If you're not interested in full-time positions with your summer employer, it's still a good idea to ask the questions—after all, this information might help your MBA colleagues back at your B-school. An exchange of this kind of information among schoolmates is also a helpful networking tool.

- Diplomatically share your thoughts with everyone about the perfect job you would like to have within your summer employer and the industry. If the role doesn't exist, find out which key stakeholders can authorize creating the role and begin talking to them about it. Let your supervisor know about these conversations because you will need his or her support. An amazing amount of opportunities can come your way if you are vocal about what it is you want.

Create Opportunities and Wiggle Room (Week 9 to the End)

The last couple of weeks will sneak away from you if you're not careful. Despite the deluge of final meetings and last-minute changes required to wrap up your project deliverables and presentations, this is the time when you need to maintain a clear focus on your objectives.

- Maintain the scope of your project(s)—read: Do not become a victim of "scope creep." As a project nears its end, people often give into the temptation to sneak in one more piece of information here and there, to add another section or two, perhaps conduct some additional analysis, or even alter the original theme of the entire body of work. This is called "scope creep"—when the scope of the work slowly creeps away from its original intent until you have a vastly larger or different project altogether. If this happens early on, there is often time to re-jigger the project, re-define its parameters, and start anew. This isn't possible in the 11th hour. If necessary, you can add a brief addendum to the project detailing the case for an additional piece of work to be completed at a later date; perhaps it could even be something you take on following your return to B-school (more on this in "Back at B-School").

- About two weeks before your last day, begin asking your supervisor and other people who make hiring decisions how, following graduation, you might step into the perfect job you've been talking about.

- Make sure you know who manages the application process for full-time positions. Talk with that manager about the recruiting schedule and any potential visits scheduled with your B-school in the upcoming academic year. Find out what you can do to best stay in touch with him or her during that time.

- From all of the conversations you've had during the summer, you've probably discovered or thought up a number of possible projects. Now's the time to turn the discussion of these projects up a notch with the groups or companies where you believe you could create or find your dream job. Begin talking about how, after your return to B-school, you could actually do some of the work you've been discussing. Based on those discussions, create a project that is as close to your dream job as possible (more on using this project information in the "Options without Internships" section).

Seal the Deal (Final Week)

With the end of your internship or summer project in sight, develop a short list of tasks to accomplish that will help ensure that all of your hard work ends with a bang, not a whimper.

- Make sure your final performance review takes place. Review your discussions about your dream job with other folks at the company. Ask your supervisor to share your performance review (it's stellar, right?) with the decision-makers, those people who may be able to create and hire you into your dream job.

- If you have a final presentation, find out if you can invite key contacts you've made at the company—these are people who have aided you in your work and who might be a future supervisor or sponsor if you return for a full-time position. If you can't invite them to your final presentation, ask if you can conduct a separate presentation for them. If this isn't do-able (some material you've worked on could be highly sensitive and confidential), at least send them a quick synopsis that your supervisor reviews prior to sending out.

- Leave personalized thank-you notes and/or voice mail messages for the people who helped you during your summer, from trouble-shooting tech support folks to admin assistants and senior executives. Make sure they understand you appreciate the hospitality and help they provided to you.

- If you're in the enviable position of receiving a verbal or formally written offer for full-time employment before your summer work is done, then you have truly made a great impression. Congratulations! Employers will most often provide you with a number of weeks or months to consider the offer. The best-case scenario involves you and your employer discussing the structure and nature of the role being offered to you in the week or weeks leading up to your departure. In this case, you do have influence over what this offer entails and tailoring that to what you think is an ideal job. Who could ask for anything more?

Back at B-School

Surrounded by the hustle and bustle of your MBA program, you will no doubt feel tempted to settle back into the defined structure imposed by your coursework. Keep a portion of you calendar clear to:

- **Stay in touch** with your key contacts back at your summer job and at other companies with whom you may have spoken.

- **Follow up** with your fellow interns and check in on their plans.

- **Maintain the conversations you started**, talking about your ideal job.

- **Start work on one of the projects** you uncovered or put together during the summer. The project should be one that allows you to get that much closer to your ideal job. You can even get credit for it if you have a faculty member and an academic advisor sign off on it as an academic practicum or independent study (see "Options without Internships" section). If the project is of a scope and magnitude that requires the effort of four to five MBAs, then a practicum is your best option. If so, you should get an appropriate faculty member involved in your thinking as soon as possible—even while you are still in the midst of your summer work. In the meantime, you can also get in touch with some colleagues from your MBA program to take part in the project with you.

Options Outside of Internships

While this guide gives advice and instruction on how to find or create, and then leverage your ideal internship, it almost begs the question, "What can be done, other than internships and summer projects, to bridge the gap between where your career has been and where you want it to go?" As a matter of fact, there are numerous ways (okay, maybe not 101) for MBA job seekers to gain tangible, marketable, and transferable experiences during their B-school career outside of formal summer internships or customized summer projects. And they can all find their way onto your resumes, into your cover letters, and become part of your conversations in order to better jumpstart your new career.

Class Projects

Almost all classes in B-school include a project of some kind. Typically, the subject matter for the project is clearly dictated by the course's syllabus and offers students little chance for customizing it to benefit their career needs. Occasionally, however, a course will allow students to create their own project to meet the academic requirements of the class. It's in these courses that a student should take full advantage of this flexibility and create a project that allows them to study, research, and investigate the industry, companies, and roles in which they have the greatest interest.

Academic Practicums

A practicum, which is typically set up by a faculty member in concert with an employer, requires a group of three to six MBAs to take on a project that has a pre-determined goal. In this case, much has been set in stone. However, a student can take the initiative to create his or her own academic practicum, one that is more tailored to his or her wants and needs. In this case, make sure a faculty member is willing to sign off on the academic merit of the project so that you can get course credit for your work.

Independent Studies

When a student has a robust, in-depth project he or she wants to take on outside of an existing course, an independent study is usually the best option. This option allows the student to complete his or her customized project and also receive academic credit. To get credit, you will need to gain signed approval from a faculty member. This means preparing for the project well in advance. A student should begin arranging his or her project idea and start requesting feedback from at least one faculty member and one career advisor (to clarify the career impact of the work) about two months before the beginning of the academic period during which he or she will get credit for the work.

An independent study is an extremely flexible tool you can use to hone your skills and bridge the gap between your past and future careers. It can be used to help you get in with multiple employers for whom you would most want to work. You can structure an independent study to give you deep exposure to a specific industry, company, product, service, technology, or process. You can and should design it to allow you to build skills, develop a network, or generate ideas and leads.

Be sure to establish a comprehensive work plan (like a syllabus) for an independent study. Doing so will help you stay on track and better manage the time and effort required to maximize the return benefits.

Self-Directed Project

If you really want full control and authority over a project aimed at enhancing your career prospects, a self-directed project may be the way to go. This type of project neither depends on an existing course nor relies on the approval of a faculty member or academic advisor. Rather, it's a project that you design and implement on your own. Such a project shouldn't simply be a networking effort or a ruse to talk to people about jobs. It should involve some rigorous research and insightful analysis.

Designing this as a real project with a framework, deadlines, and deliverables will help keep you moving forward, since this effort will be competing for your time and energy with the structured courses you are already taking. Taking steps to formalize it will make the process more meaningful to you and to your future employer. And, depending on the type of project you do, it may be possible to have a faculty member and academic advisor agree to give your academic credit for such a project after you've completed it.

Self-directed projects can be done at any time. A project such as this often works very well during the summer for individuals who have not been able to find an internship or have not created a summer project. For these students, this avenue allows them to come away with tangible and marketable experience and exposure.

For Your Reference

- Recommended Resources

- In Closing

Recommended Resources

The resources listed here are only intended as a small sampling of the information that is available to help you find and land an internship.

NACE's Job Outlook Survey

The National Association of Colleges and Employers' (NACE) *Job Outlook 2003* survey forecasts the hiring intentions of employers and examines other issues related to the employment of new college graduates. The survey is being conducted in four parts. The first part, the *Job Outlook Fall Preview*, was conducted in August 2002, and its results were released in September. The second part of the survey (includes information cited in this guide) was conducted from mid-August through September 30, 2002. Surveys were sent to 1,339 NACE employer members; 327, or 24.4 percent, responded. By type of employer, 52 percent are service-sector employers, 36.4 percent are manufacturers, and 8.2 percent are government/nonprofit employers. (An additional 3.4 percent could not be classified by sector.)

General Resources on the Web

WetFeet.com Internships. Get all of the latest information and advice.

Internships and Co-ops on JobWeb. The National Association of Colleges and Employers offers very useful resources and statistics on co-ops and internships for students on its website: www.jobweb.com.

University career center websites. Career centers at local universities often provide resources and tips for internships and much of this information is available to the public through the career center's website. (Additional services are generally reserved for current students or alumni.) For recommendations on local opportunities, look for the university in the location you are targeting for your internship. A collection of links to university career center websites in the United States, Canada, and Australia (from NACE) can be found at: www.jobweb.com/Career_Development/homepage.htm

Employer research. Learn about the companies or organizations you want to target from:

- WetFeet.com's industry and company profiles
- PR Newswire (www.prnewswire.com/news/)
- NewsDirectory.com
- Business news from 41 local markets and 46 industries (www.bizjournals.com)

Professional associations. Search information on associations in every field imaginable via the directory provided by the American Society of Association Executives (info.asaenet.org/gateway/onlineAssocslist.html) or the Internet Public Library's Database (www.ipl.org/div/aon/)

Specific Opportunities

Please note that some of the programs listed here require registration or a fee. Programs have different requirements for participation—a few are open to students only.

Business and Multiple Areas

- InternshipPrograms.com
- Rising Star Internship (www.rsinternships.com)

Internship Programs for Minority Students

- INROADS (www.inroads.org)

- Sponsors for Educational Opportunity (www.seo-ny.org)

Nonprofit and U.S. Federal Government Opportunities

- Students.gov (www.students.gov; under "Career Development," select "Internships")

- Institute for Experiential Learning (www.ielnet.org)

- Idealist/Action Without Borders (www.idealist.org)

- Environmental Career Organization (www.eco.org)

- Volunteer Match (www.volunteermatch.org)

International Programs—Internships and Work Exchange

- Association Internationale des Etudiants Sciences Economiques (AIESEC)

- Association for International Practical Training (AIPT)

- Cross-Cultural Solutions

- Council on International Educational Exchange (CIEE)

- BUNAC (British Universities North America Club)

- CDS International

- Center for International Career Development (CICD)

- International Association for the Exchange of Students for Technical Experience (IAESTE)

- Internships International

- InternAbroad.com

- Institute for International Cooperation and Development (IICD)

- USA Immigration Service website (www.usais.org/studentvisas.htm)

- Worldwide Internships and Service Education (WISE)

Resources in Print

- *Back Door Guide to Short Term Job Adventures*
- *Graduate Student's Guide to Internships and Summer Programs*
- *Internships for Dummies*
- *National Directory of Arts Internships*
- *Peterson's Internships*
- *Princeton Review Internship Bible*
- The Internship Series from the Career Education Institutes (www.internships-usa.com/books.htm)
- WetFeet *Insider Guides*
- *The Yale Daily News Guide to Internships*

In Closing

Anyone who has practiced a sport understands that, no matter the natural talent you possess, you need training and focus to win competitions. The achievements in your career are highly analogous. They require dedication, talent, a game plan, a knowledge of the playing field, coaching, and an active investment of your time and efforts. Among other things, an internship is like the essential practice before the Big Game: It's where you hone your skills and demonstrate your value to the coach and team. If you don't show up, you might sit on the bench while others are out there winning the competition. So, go out and jumpstart your career by finding or creating and then leveraging your dream internship.

About the Author

A native Texan, **Saleem Assaf** is an MBA/MPA career advisor at the McCombs School of Business (University of Texas, Austin) where he works closely with IT and operations students and their organizations, faculty, and employers. In addition to his duties in career advising, employer relations, program management, and workshop development and delivery, Saleem creates handouts and tools to help students jumpstart their new careers. His career includes roles in organizational behavior, research, and logistics with employers as varied as an Ernst & Young partnership company, ExxonMobil, and the Department of Defense Schools in Germany. Before joining the McCombs School, Saleem spent five and a half years working at Accenture in consulting and executive integration and coaching roles. It was there that he created and delivered programs and intervention tools for newly hired executives and where he first became impassioned with career development as a career. Saleem has lived or worked in England, France, Germany, and Lebanon. He received his MBA from the McCombs School. He also holds a BA in sociology and behavioral science from Rice University in Houston, Texas.

Rosanne Lurie, MS, has been a career advisor in the Bay Area for more than six years, at public and private institutions including University of California, San Francisco, and University of California, Berkeley. Her professional background includes delivery of career advising through individual counseling and workshops, as well as developing and managing Web and print resources for career center websites and libraries. In addition to orienting undergrads to career planning, she has worked with graduate students and alumni to develop their job searching skills for academic, clinical, and industry positions. A San

Francisco native, she attended Haverford College near Philadelphia and lived in the United Kingdom through a work-exchange program. She earned a master's degree in counseling from San Francisco State University, getting hired to permanent employment from an internship she participated in as part of her academic program. As a career advisor, she enjoys being available to help as her clients choose their career direction and pursue their goals.

WetFeet's Insider Guide Series

JOB SEARCH GUIDES

Getting Your Ideal Internship

Job Hunting A to Z: Landing the Job You Want

Killer Consulting Resumes!

Killer Investment Banking Resumes!

Killer Cover Letters & Resumes!

Negotiating Your Salary & Perks

Networking Works!

INTERVIEW GUIDES

Ace Your Case: Consulting Interviews

Ace Your Case II: 15 More Consulting Cases

Ace Your Case III: Practice Makes Perfect

Ace Your Case IV: The Latest & Greatest

Ace Your Case V: Return to the Case Interview

Ace Your Interview!

Beat the Street: Investment Banking Interviews

Beat the Street II: I-Banking Interview Practice Guide

CAREER & INDUSTRY GUIDES

Careers in Accounting

Careers in Advertising & Public Relations

Careers in Asset Management & Retail Brokerage

Careers in Biotech & Pharmaceuticals

Careers in Brand Management

Careers in Consumer Products

Careers in Entertainment & Sports

Careers in Human Resources

Careers in Information Technology

Careers in Investment Banking

Careers in Management Consulting

Careers in Manufacturing

Careers in Marketing & Market Research

Careers in Nonprofits & Government Agencies

Careers in Real Estate

Specialized Consulting Careers: Health Care, Human Resources &
Information Technology

Careers in Supply Chain Management

Careers in Venture Capital

Consulting for PhDs, Doctors & Lawyers

Industries & Careers for MBAs

Industries & Careers for Undergrads

COMPANY GUIDES

Accenture

Bain & Company

Boston Consulting Group

Booz Allen Hamilton

Citigroup's Corporate & Investment Bank

Credit Suisse First Boston

Deloitte Consulting

Goldman Sachs Group

J.P. Morgan Chase & Company

Lehman Brothers

McKinsey & Company

Merrill Lynch

Morgan Stanley

25 Top Consulting Firms

Top 20 Biotechnology & Pharmaceuticals Firms

Top 25 Financial Services Firms